How to Sell Life Insurance 2nd edition

Life Insurance Selling Techniques, Tips and Strategies

Written by Michael Bonilla, CPCU

Copyright 2019

"Everyone has a plan, until they get punched in the mouth." – Mike Tyson

About the Author

Believe it or not this section is always the hardest for me to write about. I really don't enjoy talking about myself. I enjoy having people talk about themselves. What do people want to know about an author? Background? Experiences? Belief systems? I enjoy breaking things and putting them back together. What kind of person am I? What kind of person do I want to represent?

Let me tell you a brief story that tells you what kind of person I am. Back in the early 90's I was sketching out my design for a boxcar derby car for boy scouts. This was my first race and I couldn't think of the type of car I wanted to build. To say the least there was zero inspiration. I scribbled out some designs on this piece of paper and eventually after running out of paper went into the den to find more paper. I stopped for a second and glanced over by the window. After staring out of the window for a second (maybe several minutes) I saw my father as he was pulling into the driveway with his 1990 White Dodge diesel, you could hear it for miles.

Then it hit me. What if I used his truck as the

design? I re-read the instructions and rules for the derby. The boxcar kit came in a small cardboard box with a block of wood we could use to make our cars. The instructions read as follows:

* Must have 4 wheels
* Must weigh X LBs, no more and no less.
* Must be X inches long by X Inches wide.

So, that being said. Nowhere in the rules/instructions did it specifically say "this boxcar must be a car". So, for the first time in the boxcar derby history. Michael Bonilla entered a truck. To which everyone started laughing. It was a small wooded version of a 1990's Dodge Ram 2500. With a big Pepsi decal on the driver side door. So, we called it the Pepsi truck.

I placed my 'car' on the race line for the first race and hoped for the best. The judges looked at it. It met the weight requirements, the size requirements and had the appropriate amount of wheels. So, we raced and I waited with anticipation for the results. As I was short I couldn't even see the race. All I heard was, "Pepsi truck 1st place." After all 5 races that day I kept hearing those same words over and over again.

After sweeping that year's event. The following year I decided to change it up and make a replica of the Mach 5 Speed Racer Car, in which I came in third place. That next year every 'car' was a truck, besides mine. Don't bend the rules, don't break the rules, test the rules and test the boundaries of the game you are given. Look for loopholes and exploits in the system.

I'm unsure what kind of insight that might have provided. Nevertheless, this book is the longest, most through and probably well thought out I have written to date. I'm an author, a consultant, a former agency owner, an avid golfer, a husband and most importantly someone who enjoys giving back through teaching.

Preface

In this second edition of 'How to Sell Life Insurance' you will find more tips, tricks and processes to help move the dial in your life insurance practice. Hundreds of years ago when the first life insurance policy was written, it was written without an insurance agent present. For another hundred or so years ago we managed to live without insurance agents. Believe it or not when insurance agents entered the picture they did so unlicensed for about 75 years! Our industry is an old industry and rapidly evolving. By in large agents will exist for many years to come, because 75% of consumers have to be prompted by a person to pursue a life quote. As long as we can add value in the supply chain, agents will hold a strong foothold in the financial services space.

This book is not a one-size fits all solution to every possible sales situation. My intention with this book, my goal with this book if you will is to give you a spark of inspiration. I'm not here to tell you what to think and I'm not here to tell you how to think, I'm simply here to give you something interesting to think about. If you're looking for all the answers this is not the book. This is more of a framework, guidebook and some useful questions/tips.

All that being said, take some time to think about why you bought this book. Was it the blue cover? Was it the book or was it the wanting for something to take from the book. Is there something holding you back in your current practice? Finding it tough to convert in this modern age of life sales? What is your reason for doing what you do?

Contents

About the Author 5
Preface 9
Part 1: Introduction & Basics 16
Chapter 1: Introduction 18
    Emotional Sale 20
    What do people really buy when they purchase a life insurance policy? 23
    What business are we in? 23
    Brief History 24
    Takeaway from this book 24
Chapter 2: Life Sale Basics 28
    But Mike, What if I don't know how to ask open ended questions? 29
    But Mike, how do I show someone I care? How do I get someone engaged in the process? 32
    But Mike, nobody wants to sit down and talk about life insurance, right? 34
    But Mike, what if I sell on the phone/email? 35
    Telling is not selling! 36
    Reasons for buying life insurance 37
Chapter 3: Life Insurance Basics 44
    But Mike, What if I don't know how to answer to a question? 44
    Facts about Life Insurance 45
   Types of Life Insurance 46
   Endorsements 48

But Mike, What if my company doesn't offer those endorsements?..49

Option Riders..49

Addition Riders..50

Expediting Riders..50

Part 2: Life Sales Fundamental Info..53

Chapter 4: Selling You, Selling Your Process, Selling Your Product and Selling Your Company...........................55

Selling You..56

My Process..58

Selling Your Story..60

But Mike, What if I don't have a personal story/connection as to why I sell life insurance?.........63

Selling Your Product..63

But Mike, What if my product sucks?..65

Selling Your Company..65

But Mike, what if my company sucks?..66

Chapter 5: Objection Handling..69

Game Theory and Selling..70

But Mike, what if they keep asking about price and rate?..71

Why is this person shopping?..75

How do I beat a cheap policy?..75

Objection to Application. Generic objection...........................76

Common Objection; I don't need life insurance, I have a policy through work..77

Common Objection: "I think I need to ask my wife or spouse."..78

- Setting the Stage ... 80
- Why do Client's Object? ... 81
- Preempting the Objection ... 82
- The Art of Pausing ... 83
- Forgetting to ask Please ... 84
- Insurance Doctor ... 84
- Tips to Avoid Objections / General Selling Tips ... 85

Chapter 6: Consultative Selling, Transactional Selling and Relationship Based Selling. ... 89

- What is Consultative Selling? ... 89
- What is Transactional Selling? ... 89
- What is Relationship Based Selling? ... 90
- But Mike, Don't people have to like me if they want to do business with me? ... 90
- What do you focus on? ... 90
- Consultative Strategies ... 91
- Transactional Strategies ... 92
- Ending Note ... 93

Chapter 7: Other Considerations ... 96

- Replacement Life Policy Strategies ... 96
- But Mike, What if my client has a bad policy? ... 96
- 401K vs IUL/VUL: Comparing Insurance to Investment Accounts ... 97
- Life Insurance Retirement Plan ... 97
- But Mike, that sounds too good to be true... ... 98
- But Mike, this sounds too good to be true, what's the catch? ... 100
- Downfalls of Indexed Universal Life Insurance. ... 100

- Pension Maximization 101
- How do you talk about you? 103
- Selling on Value vs Selling on Price. 103
- But Mike, What if my policies keep cancelling? 106
- How do I get a referral partner to reciprocate? 106

Part 3: Sales Process 108

Chapter 8: Prospecting / Active Marketing Plans 110
- What is prospecting? 111
- But Mike, I'm not interesting and I have a hard time meeting people in networking groups 111
- Ideas for Marketing Activities 112
- Life Insurance Triggering Events 117
- Transitioning Statements 118
- General Rapport Building Advice 119

Chapter 9: The First Presentation (Define the Benefit/Product and Submit Application) 122
- But Mike, How do I make a persuasive presentation? 122
- Opening questions 123
- But Mike, How do I Determine a client's Death Benefit? 124
- But Mike, Why these systems? 127
- L.I.F.E – The life conversation is a simple way to determine a client's death benefit. 127
- Personal Balance Sheet Approach 131
- Needs Analysis and Qualifying Process 132
- But Mike, my company is just not competitive on price... 133

    But Mike, Shouldn't I ask about the Person's budget for life insurance?..........134

    Other Qualifying Questions 134

    Building a Qualifying Process..........135

    Product Selection...........136

    Farmer Analogy and Bucket Strategy 136

    Sell the Medical Exam...........137

    But Mike, if I don't give them a quote how do I know how much to put down for the down payment on the conditional insurance?..........141

    Good, Better and Best: The Red Herring of Sales..........141

    How do I know when to present Perm over Term?...141

    Some questions to ponder: 142

    But Mike, how do I know when I'm in rapport with a client? 142

    Closing Questions..........144

Chapter 10: The Last Presentation: Presenting the offer from the insurance company. 146

    Closing the Sale. 149

Chapter 11: Summation..........150

Appendix of Questions 151

    Prospecting Questions..........151

    Transitioning Questions 151

    Opening Questions 151

    Needs Analysis Questions 152

    Closing Questions..........153

Other Books 154

Part 1: Introduction & Basics

"Quality is not an act, it is a habit." - Aristotle

Chapter 1: Introduction

Have you ever written a policy so large that you sat back in your chair and said to yourself, "This is going to be a good month." It's a great feeling, how long does it last? There's a flip side to that coin. Have you ever found yourself staring at the phone waiting for it to ring? Because, apparently for some reason unbeknownst to me, nobody in the entire United States of America that day wanted to buy life insurance.

The reason I wrote this book is to help Agents find better ways to be more consistent, confident and competent. Why? Tom Landry said it best, "The secret to winning is constant, consistent management." I'd like to help you be more consistent in your processes, more consistent in your underwriting and just more consistent in getting to the finish line.

When I think of selling life insurance, it's actually a lot like baseball. For me growing up I was never the home run hitter. But, I was consistent in getting on base. Why? Because, I knew as a smaller kid the outfield would 'scoot in' and by that happening, I could hit a pop-up line drive that went right over their heads into the outfield. I couldn't hit the ball over the fence, but I could hit it just over the second baseman's reach into the outfield. That was my system for getting on base.

Ever watch baseball today? Some batters tend to only swing for the fences and end up striking out a lot. But, they also end up hitting home runs. When you look at the last world series, it was won on fundamental baseball and not just swinging for the fences. I grew up playing ball in the times of McGwire, Bonds, and Sosa... Hitting home runs were everything back then.

The game is somewhat more nuanced now. It's about getting back to basic fundamentals. Getting on base. Being a more consistent player. Knowing what you're good at and more importantly knowing what you are not good at. Mitigating risk by not stealing bases. Throwing the guy out at first and not second or third. To put it simply, by not making mistakes that lose the 'sale'.

I wrote this book to help you learn how to just

get on base. Don't get me wrong, the home runs will come. The key to successful life sales is just that. Your ability to get on base. I'm not saying don't swing for the fences. I'm saying to become a great life sales person... first learn to be consistent. In this book we will cover tips, systems and techniques to help you increase your odds of making the sale. I'd like to share a valuable piece of advice that my father (a carpenter by trade) taught me when I was about 5 years old. He said, "Mike... measure twice and cut once."

Emotional Sale

Have you ever heard people say that life insurance is an emotional sale? The key difference from what separates a great life agent and a price driven life agent, is the ability to tether a life insurance policy with personal experiences of the insured or emotions. How do you make this policy meaningful to the prospect? How do you attach it to feelings? A life insurance sale is a search for the truth. The truth is that everyone needs life insurance, but for many different reasons and during different stages of life.

So, what makes life insurance an emotional

sale? As an agent you need to learn three things about every client:

- Where your client has been. (Past Experiences)
- Where they are now. (Current Financial Situation)
- Where they are going. (Goal Setting for retirement Planning)

Everyone has a family member that has passed away prematurely or suffered from a serious illness. Let's look at it another way. When a breadwinner for a family passes away, the spouse now is thrust into single parenthood and becomes the breadwinner by proxy. What does that mean for the spouse? It depends on what the spouse has been doing?

- Do they have to re-enter the workforce?
- Do they have to learn how to file taxes?
- Do they have to learn how to budget or balance a check book?
- Do they have to decide between paying the mortgage and a funeral?

- Do they have limited time to make important decisions?

In this book we will cover a comprehensive approach to selling life insurance, everything from creating a process to answering common objections. The first thing to learn is that life Insurance is a front loaded process. That is to say, the majority of our work is done before an offer is made by the insurance company to the insured.

Have you noticed that the insurance industry is starting to become more and more commoditized. Investment banks sure have. Why? It's mostly due to bad sales strategies by agents and or price gauging. Most agents sell insurance based on the rate and the rate they can offer is the value they can provide. Back in the day, when there was 1 insurance agent in your small town, having market access was a big deal. Before the existence of this little thing called… the internet, that might have been a great strategy for some Agents. But, now more than ever value in life sales comes from customizing your offering, educating and advising.

What do people really buy when they purchase a life insurance policy?

They are buying a promise. They are buying peace of mind. God forbid they should walk out of your office and get hit by a bus, their family would be taken care of financially. This business has been and always will be for the most part a relationship business. What does a person buy? You either sell them on a compelling vision for the future or they sell you on a reason why they don't need life insurance. Don't forget it!

What business are we in?

What business are we in? Have you ever thought about it? Well, Mike we are in the business of selling life insurance, right? We are in the business of selling peace of mind. We are in the trust business. Okay, well you're just going to tell me to sell the value like every corporate rep, sales consultant or person from management. To which I say, when you are not the cheapest or significantly cheaper, what value do you really add to the process? When you lose on price, what is your plan? Artificial intelligence will do a much better job at price shopping than we can ever hope to do as agents. When a client walks into your office with a cheaper quote, what's your plan? From my experience 'hoping for the best' is not a reliable business level strategy.

Brief History

The first life insurance contract was written hundreds of years ago and the industry remained relatively small for centuries. Fast forward to 2014 and we have the largest policy ever written coming in around $200,000,000. For years life insurance agents had ZERO licensure requirements and very little regulation around selling insurance policies. Today an insured can purchase insurance from a website, from a broker or agent and possibly on their smartphone. Technology has shaped our industry and is evolving along consumer habits.

Takeaway from this book...

The main take away from this book is that selling is an odds game and selling requires a lot of deductive reasoning. Selling is all about the odds. How do we increase your odds of closing a sale? It's actually quite simple. We start by increasing the number of applications you are submitting. The law of large numbers. Throughout this book we will focus on ways to do just that.

For instance, if you meet with a prospect in-person your odds dramatically increase compared to emailing quotes or selling over the phone. How insightful, right? Having a consistent process will increase your odds of selling, because responses and objections are somewhat predictable based on your approach. Using a proper needs analysis to determine the death benefit will increase your odds. Asking open ended questions and follow up questions will increase your odds as it will help you gather more information on the prospect. Leveraging endorsements based on that information gathered will increase your odds as you have a customized offering that links a personally identified need from the prospect. Not quoting premium figures and learning to sell the Medical Exam before discussing numbers will increase your odds of selling as well. Developing a proper qualifying process will help you increase your odds of success.

An ending note, although meeting in person is

rather old school, it works. People tend to spend time or invest time in and with things we care about.

All growth depends upon activity. There is no development physically or intellectually without effort, and effort means work. – Calvin Coolidge

Chapter 2: Life Sale Basics

Purchasing life insurance isn't like purchasing a bar of soap at your local grocery store. There should be a good amount of planning, consideration and thought that comes along with the purchase. A Life Insurance sale has a somewhat lengthy process for the most part. Later on in the book we will talk about this in more detail.

Here is a simple outline:

1. Prospecting/Qualifying (Pre-underwriting)
2. Educating/Needs Analysis/Application Submittal (Field Underwriting/Medical)
3. Offer Review/Policy Issuance (Post Underwriting)

Prospecting, Qualifying and building rapport is all predicated on your ability to ask questions. By asking questions you are able to get someone's attention and generate interest. But, more importantly asking open ended questions and specific questions. How secure do you think the stock market is? In retirement what would you say most worries you?

But Mike, What if I don't know how to ask open ended questions?

Don't worry I'll have specific examples in this book to help you.

Once you're able to gather enough interest from the prospect, then and only then does the real learning process begin. Remember, you never stop building rapport during the sale. It's not a one and done exercise, it's a dynamic process throughout the entirety of the sale. Rapport building is something you have to continually work on, even throughout the relationship of the client.

The best way to garner interest is by discovering a solution for a possible problem or challenge the prospect is facing. To discover a solution we must first uncover an underlying problem. This entails outlining determining a death benefit or a need. Or in simple language, "What happens to your family should god forbid you walk out of this office and get his by a bus?"

After you determine the death benefit and design a product to fulfill the benefit, then you submit an application. My theory for life sales is simple. Focus on education, don't quote number and the more applications you submit to qualified prospects the more sales you make. Simple, right?

Whether selling on price or value, playing the law of large numbers is the key to success with life insurance. I'll explain the strategy in more detail throughout the book, but it comes down the key principles of compliance science. The more you can get a prospect to be agreeable and say 'yes' throughout the process, the more likely you will get to the finish line.

The first major commitment is asking the prospect to sit down with you for a meeting. It's not a large commitment, but a commitment none the less. After you have sat down and done a proper needs analysis you are asking for an even larger commitment, a medical exam and conditional receipt of insurance. You're asking them to commit to an amount of insurance as well. Once an offer is made by the insurance company all of those past commitments will have built up to hopefully just push you over the finish line.

I'll break this down later on in the book. But, what it boils down to is that through the process the prospect really does the majority of the work and takes a large ownership stake in the process. Think of it like a bunch of mini-closes to build to a larger close. How you present also makes a big difference. For the most part people are visual learners. So, do yourself a favor and illustrate for your clients. Use a white board or a note pad to show them what you are talking about. If you rely on numbers in your presentation then write them down in front of the prospect, so you can easily reference them. For instance, if you determine a death benefit write down a step by step process.

Have you heard the old phrase telling is not selling? It's the hardest lesson to learn as a new life insurance agent. You can rattle on about product knowledge and how indexed universal life insurance is the best retirement solution since sliced bread, but the truth is that no one cares. At least they won't care how much you know until they know how much you care. Caring is infectious, it's like a drug, people want to be validated and cared about.

But Mike, how do I show someone I care? How do I get someone engaged in the process?

Learn the art of asking open ended questions. If you want to get people engaged in a subject you have to ask questions in your presentation. Have you ever sat through an Indexed Universal Life Insurance presentation and start thinking about ways to the nearest exit?

A couple of years ago I sat through a 45 minute IUL presentation. The rep was explaining the product in so much detail that even I got bored. In-between spewing out life insurance benefits and market facts the rep wouldn't let me get a word in edge wise. Other than to ask me if that made sense. Few things to think about:

1. Ordinary people don't like being barraged with life insurance information.
2. Ordinary people don't like being interrogated. Ask important questions.
3. Don't placate people with questions to further your presentation or to just get a 'yes' for the sake of getting a yes.
4. Ordinary people don't want to understand every little detail of an insurance policy.

Remember not to ask questions just to check a box. This is a conversation not an interview. Also, I see a lot of new Agents focus too much on education and end up drowning a prospect in information and factoids. Although you will have a structure or a process, experience is what will teach you when to ask certain questions and in what order. Experience will also teach you when to ask follow ups and how to pause. Don't forget to not answer your own questions and when you ask a question, shut up and wait for an answer.

Once you ask a question... wait for the prospect to answer! I can't tell you how many presentations I've watched where the Agent asks the prospect a question. And just as the prospect begins to think or utter an answer, the Agent chimes in with the answer. Don't let your uncomfortableness with the awkward silence outweigh your ability to actively listen. Even if the prospect comes back with the wrong answer, let them answer the question! It's called the law of reciprocity, learn it.

Another aspect of insurance sales that people commonly overlook is attitude. I'm not talking about just having a positive mental attitude and thinking good thoughts. I'm talking about the balance between caring and not caring too much. There is a level of desperation that a client can intuitively pick up on if you come across as too desperate. You have to care, fundamentally, but not too much. You'll find the right balance and it may sound a little silly at first but one day you'll understand exactly what I'm talking about.

I thought I'd touch a bit on presentation style and method here. Most people communicate now electronically. So, as a rule of thumb I would do what others are not doing. Because, there is less competition and you can go in and dominate a space. For instance, I would never send a quote over email or relay it on a call. I would always transition into setting up a face to face appointment.

> But Mike, nobody wants to sit down and talk about life insurance, right?

Wrong. A person about to sign up for a $3,000,000 life insurance policy is going to want to know how it works. But, more so face to face appointments will increase the odds of you closing the sale. One, it's a lot easier to say "no" over the phone, than it is in person and furthermore if you sit down with someone it shows they actually care about the subject.

We've all had those situations where someone calls in for a term quote, you provide a quick quote without obtaining a lot of detailed information and that's the last time you ever hear from them. Instead of just spewing out non-binding numbers, I would always focus on setting up an appointment to dig down into the numbers and needs of prospect. If someone calls in for a quote take the mentality that, I can put any number out there, but it means nothing until the medical is done.

But Mike, what if I sell on the phone/email?

Great. Do what works for you and what is consistent with your overall process. For me to see any tangible results, I met with clients face to face with people. Ask your management team. Face to face appointments result in a much higher conversation ratio, but it's much more time consuming.

Telling is not selling!

Our job is not to tell people what to think or how to think. Our job as sales people is to give them something to think about and transform their way of thinking. Which involves us planting seeds and letting those ideas grow throughout the client life cycle. My job is not to convince you I am right and you are wrong, it's to convince you that my idea is your idea. You can enumerate benefits all day long until the cow comes home but product knowledge doesn't sell insurance.

Telling: Here's why you need life insurance.

Selling: By the way who do you have your life insurance with?

Telling: Let's sit down to talk about life insurance.

Selling: Now that we've covered your home/auto, when can we carve out some time to protect your most valuable assets?

Telling: You've gotta have life insurance.

Telling: John, you have a lot of toys (RV, Bike, etc.), you should really get life insurance.

Selling: John, we've insured all your toys, but why isn't your most valuable asset protected? What's stopping you from protecting your family against financial ruin?

Telling: John, you should really think about getting a Long Term Care insurance rider on your life policy, because In-Home Nursing care can be really expensive.

Selling: John, do you know anyone who has had to go into nursing care or a nursing home? What do you think that costs? Roughly. Let me ask you something, is that something you want coverage for?

Reasons for buying life insurance.

Why do people buy life insurance? Do they buy it because of a price or because of an unmet urgent need to protect their families and assets? Life insurance is by in large an emotional purchase, it starts in the heart and close with logical reasoning.

Income replacement – Loss of a bread winner can devastate a family's ability to maintain their current lifestyle, not to mention the emotional trauma. Even loss of a spouse who doesn't earn income can be financially burdensome. Think of all the work your spouse does in the background that would now be a cost.

Funeral Expenses – What are typical funeral expenses? They vary wildly. But, you may need a plot, tombstone, funeral service, etc. Some estimates are $20,000. This is one of the easiest ways to start a dialogue with a prospect. Why? Because, most likely they had to bury a loved one and pay the bill or see the bill. Did you know the crypt above Marilyn Monroe sold for over $1,000,000? Food for thought.

Outstanding Debt Repayment – Most people have some form of either credit card debt or student loans that they leave behind after passing away. The average mortgage is around $190,000 in America. The average American holds around $16,000 in credit card debt. The average American who has student loans holds up to $48,000 in debt. The average American who has a car loan has a loan of $28,000.

Estate Tax Planning – The most efficient way to

mitigate estate taxes is with the use of permanent life insurance. When Financial Advisors say there is no need for permanent life insurance, I say they don't understand how Estate Taxes work. For a single person estate over $5.5M taxes can be upward of 40% and the IRS requires payment within 9 months of the owner passing away. Consult with an Estate Attorney for the details. You want your heirs, not the government to inherit your wealth, right? (This might be out of date)

Buy/Sell Agreement – When you have a partnership it's common in a continuation plan to have a Buy/Sell in place and funding that Buy/Sell with a life insurance policy.

Education Funding – Leaving money for a child of grandchild can be a motivating factor for some clients. The amount of money needed will vary wildly on which school and age of child.

Business Continuation Plan – Life insurance can be used to fund a buy/sell agreement for business partners. Also, Cross Sell arrangements.

Key Person Life – Life policies can be used to hire a

replacement for a Key employee, if lost due to death. In a nut shell, a company purchases an insurance policy on a Key Employee. The company is the payer of the premium, the owner of the policy and the beneficiary. If that Key Person should pass away unexpectedly, then the company would be able to hire someone immediately or implement a support structure.

Charitable gift – An under used life insurance selling strategy is portioning some or all of a life insurance death benefit to a charity. An insured can actually write off the premiums as a donation to the charity if set up correctly. A charity can be the owner of a life insurance contract on the donor based on historical donation given (usually). The donor can pay the charity and the charity can take those donations to pay the premium.

Mortgage Protection – Mortgage Protection is one of the oldest simplest ways to approach a death benefit. In my opinion part of being a responsible homeowner is owning life insurance.

Retirement Planning – An essential part of any retirement plan is a healthy amount of life insurance.

Life insurance can be geared towards building cash value and liquidating some or all of the cash value during retirement. Life Insurance can be a great way to mitigate heavy tax penalties in a retirement plan.

Child Life Insurance – Believe it or not the largest whole life producer in the country has usually been those small Gerber grow up plans. Small child policies cost pennies per day and can accumulate cash value over time. I wanted to take a little extra time and talk about Child life policies and they are important.

We had a client who turned down a child life policy on his young son. About three months later his son died in a fatal car crash and we had to have a tough conversation. So, what happened? This client became a walking talking reason for juvenile life insurance. When we're young we sort of take life for granted and think we're invincible, but we also need to hold a sobering reminder as to the fragility of life. This will always be one of the most underserved markets, because no parent should ever have to consider suffering from an event like this.

Advanced Markets – Advanced market cases often require the input from CPA's, attorneys and or other key stakeholders for the Insured. An advanced market case is any premium over $10,000 per year and usually involves more complicated strategies. Such as, IRA bequest and Wealth replacement trusts, charitable remainder trusts, maximizing IRA assets to heirs, maximizing B trusts, Pension Maximization, etc. If your carrier or TPA provides point of sales support it is usually worth it for these cases as your close rate is higher and the premium allotted usually adjusts up.

"Fear is the greatest obstacle to learning. But fear is your best friend. Fear is like fire. If you learn to control it, you let it work for you. If you don't learn to control it, it'll destroy you and everything around you." – Cus D'amato

Chapter 3: Life Insurance Basics.

What you'll learn in this section:

1. Life Insurance Factoids.
2. Life Insurance Basic Coverage Concepts and Endorsements.
3. Reasons why people purchase Life Insurance.

Knowledge is not power, it's the key to unlocking power. I implore you to learn your craft. The foundation of a good life practice is knowledge and the ability to relay that knowledge in a meaningful way. If you want to be taken seriously make sure to know your stuff. People who are interested in what you are offering will most likely have some questions.

But Mike, What if I don't know how to answer to a question?

I don't care if you have twenty years' experience, an alphabet soup of acronyms next to your name and or have qualified for MDRT ten years in a row, there will be questions you can't answer. It's going to happen. You'd be surprised what you don't know, until you know what you don't know.

Remember, the average prospect aka most people know very little about life insurance. If you don't know the answer be the kind of person who is always willing to find it. Just be honest and assure them you will find an answer.

Facts about Life Insurance

1. 40% of People Have No Life Insurance.
2. 25% of Households Don't Have Enough Life Insurance.
3. 80% of Shoppers Overestimate the Cost of Life Insurance.
4. Average Death Benefit is around $165,000.
5. About 95% of term policy holders outlive their term.
6. The Median Salary for a Life Agent is $48,000.
7. The cost of a Life Only License is about $190.
8. The turnover rate among Life Agents is 93% the first year.
9. When you search 'life insurance' over 415,000,000 results show up on search engines.

10. Average life expectancy is around 80 years old in the United States, and has been going down.

Types of Life Insurance

Permanent Life: Permanent life insurance falls into two categories. Either a client can purchase a whole life insurance policy or a more flexible universal life insurance policy.

Whole Life Insurance: Whole life offers fixed premiums, a fixed rate of interest that builds cash value, a fixed death benefit, and some policies pay dividends. The most common type of whole life insurance is Final Expense Whole Life.

Universal Life Insurance: Universal policies can be fixed or variable, accumulate cash value, and death benefits can increase or remain level of time.

Types of Universal Life Insurance: Variable Universal Life Insurance and Indexed Universal Life Insurance are the most popular forms of Universal policies.

Advantages: Part of your money pays the cost of insurance and part earns interest which can accumulate cash value. You can borrow against the policies cash value. (Note) Some life needs can only be met with universal life insurance.

Disadvantages: More costly than Term Insurance. The cost of insurance usually increases each year requiring the insured to pay higher costs year over year to fund the policy. Interest rates are usually not guaranteed. Universal policies have surrender charges and usually within the first 10 years before an insured can break even.

Term Life. Term or Temporary insurance runs for a designated term aka length of time. Term Lengths: 1, 5, 10, 15, 20, 25, or 30 year term lengths.

Types of Term Life Insurance: Guaranteed Level Term, Decreasing Term Life, Single Year Term Life, and Return of Premium Term Life.

Advantages: The overall cost of insurance less expensive than permanent insurance. Most term policies are guaranteed level premium payments. Term policies can also be renewal or convertible into permanent insurance. Return of Premium Term policies return the premium to the policy holder upon maturity of the term policy, assuming the insured person lives. For most people and for most life insurance needs, term can be a viable option as a potential funding mechanism.

Disadvantages: On average about 95% of term policy holders outlive their policy. Term Insurance accumulates zero cash value. Many consultative life strategies cannot be fulfilled solely by term insurance. Endorsements for policies go away after the policy lapses or cancels or non-renews and may not be available for repurchase. After age 75 term insurance is almost impossible to obtain.

Endorsements

Have you had someone you know suffer from dementia or a stroke? Have you had someone you know end up in hospice care? We all have or know someone who knows someone who has and odds are that your prospect has as well. Endorsements are great and easy ways to customize an insurance offering for each client's specific needs. Riders generally fall into three categories; Options, Additions, and Expediting. (These aren't industry terms I just made them up for categorical purposes)

But Mike, What if my company doesn't offer those endorsements?

Most companies offer endorsements. Whatever you have, learn it. Don't be afraid to say you don't know. Say that you'll look into it while we...

Option Riders

Option Riders are riders that provide options at certain time periods. For instance, the option to purchase additional insurance.

Guaranteed Insurability Rider - This rider allows you to purchase additional insurance coverage along with your base policy in the stated period without the need for further medical examination. This rider may end at a specified age.

Guaranteed Renewable – This rider allows a policy holder to purchase another policy at the end of the term regardless of medical underwriting changes.

Convertible Period – Convertibility can make a huge difference between the value of term policies.

Some term companies will allow a policy holder to convert anytime during the policy period to a permanent. A typical cut off period is within 10 to 14 years depending on the policy type.

Addition Riders

Addition Riders are riders that allow you to purchase additional benefits or second to die contracts or multiple life contracts.

Second to Die: Second to die contracts are life policies that cover two people. For instance, you can have a contract that covers both spouses.

Child Life Addition: Many term and permanent contracts allow an insured the option before purchase to buy a small term life policy attached as a rider to their policy.

Expediting Riders

Expediting Riders allow a client to expedite benefits when there is a triggering event. For example, a long term care option or Disability Waiver of Premium option.

Premium Waiver: Premium waivers are a huge

selling point if you are able to sell them. It grants the payer of the premium to forego paying premium if they are severely ill.

LTC – Long Term Care was once a thriving standalone insurance market and now has pivoted as the fastest growing life endorsement. The LTC allows an insured to use their death benefit or part of their death benefit in the event they need in-bed nursing care due to not being able to complete "Activities of Daily Living". LTC standalone policies normally have long elimination periods that can cause the insured to self-insure a lot of cost. With an LTC rider normally that elimination period is shorter or non-existent.

Disability: Disability works much in the way of a standard premium waiver. It grants the payer the ability to forgo paying premiums if they become disabled. Some disability riders can expedite a death benefit and cover some of the costs of disability.

Critical Illness Rider: Critical Illness Riders are riders that allow the insured the ability to liquidate the death benefit or part of the death benefit during the term.

>Usually illnesses trigger an elimination period of 90 days and then benefits can be allotted. For example, a major life ending illness can trigger benefits to be allocated to the insured.

Part 2: Life Sales Fundamental Info

"Social action, just like physical action, is steered by perception." - Kurt Lewin.

Chapter 4: Selling You, Selling Your Process, Selling Your Product and Selling Your Company.

Prospects need to have absolute certainty that you are an expert in your field, an authority on your subject matter, and that you are credible enough to buy something from. Remember Bob Burg, 'All things being equal people tend to do business with people they know, like and trust.' So, how do you build that certainty?

1. You must be able to sell Yourself.
2. Sell your Process.
3. Sell Your Product.
4. Sell your Company.

If you can set the stage properly and educate the client on these aspects of your practice, it will greatly reduce the number of objections you receive from prospects.

I've heard from a lot reps that, "Oh I'm a great sales person." Or "My closing rate is 90%." But, when I ask them to explain their sales process or draw it on a while board I usually get a blank stare.

Most Agents tend to stumble into sales without understanding how they got there or understand how they connect with clients. The key is not to overwhelm them with information, but to have a process or system you can rely on.

Selling You.

How do you sell yourself to someone else? What do you do really well? What do you do that makes you stand out from the competition? Do you take orders and merely price shop for the lowest possible rate? Are you a trusted advisor that actually takes time to educate clients and add value?

Remember as insurance agents we are not creators of things, we uncover needs and discover solutions to challenges facing clients. Part of learning to sell you involves developing your Unique Value Proposition or more commonly known as the elevator pitch. How do you describe yourself to other people? Usually when I ask agents, I get one of two broad answers:

- **Transactional Agent:** I Sell Life Insurance by shopping the market for the best rate.

- **Consultative Agent:** I provide peace of mind to middle class families by educating them about their assets exposed to loss. We do that by making customized recommendations to protect their assets/families.

(Remember) Enthusiasm and charisma will only get you so far in selling. You need to provide value, be creative.

Selling 'You' also involves explaining Your Process. It takes some time to develop a process that is congruent with your flow. There is no perfect process for selling Life Insurance that will allow you to close 100% of your sales. But, having a process will be the difference for achieving consistent success in your career. What is a selling point a small business have that a large doesn't? The ability to be nimble and agile. As a client you get me. You get my cell phone, if there is a question you can call me. Plus, our agency is local and there isn't a 1-800 that we pawn you off to.

Ask yourself, why you? Why should this person listen to you? Why should they buy from you? There are 1,000,000 licensed insurance professionals in the U.S.A., so why you?

My Process

My process was rather simplistic. During my process we would condense the sale into three distinctive parts that I molded loosely around the CPCU/CLU model. We would do three things Educate, Build a Custom Proposal and make our professional recommendation.

For example, "Let me walk you through my process and my process is somewhat detailed. But, what I found is that if we can answer your questions and address any concerns you may have about life insurance it makes the buying process more comfortable." Or, "What we do is three things. We educate to answer any possible questions and explain how the insurance works, then we customize the insurance to fit your specific situation and then we make our professional recommendation."

Breaking the process down into distinct phases helps your customer grasp what you are trying to accomplish. I've also found people tend to think in threes, so having a three step process made sense.

(This process is broadly modeled after the CPCU/CLU sales process, invest in your education)

During the Education Phase we would flush out questions and concerns and use that as an opportunity to educate. This is the needs analysis and bridges into the product design. We spend time properly qualifying each prospect and designing a program to specifically meet their situation. Education is the cornerstone of any consultative sales process.

During the Recommendation phase. We make our professional recommendation based on the client's specific needs. We make the conversation about their number, not our number. We fit the coverage to best meet the client's goals and budget.

During the Customizing phase. Obviously not every client goes thru with our recommendation sometimes we need to make adjustments. Sometimes they want more insurance and sometimes less. Sometimes they wouldn't want to budget what would make them at 100% of the LIFE calculation and or they wanted some blended approach.

Creating your process is as important as any other part of the sale. Your process really helps you stand out as an expert in the field and an authority on your subject. Figure out a process that works for you.

Selling Your Story.

A much overlooked part of 'Selling You' is the ability to have some personal connection to the importance of owning life insurance. Life Insurance is an emotional purchase and connecting emotion into your presentation is crucial to selling on value.

It was Friday morning December 6th 2013 the first meeting of the month for my Rotary club. The mood was a little dampened compared to our normal cheery ambience. As we all sat down for our normal morning breakfast and presentation, something was kind of off.

A young woman walked to the podium and began to tell us her story. She was a recently widowed mother of two. She mustered enough courage to not cry as she held up a jar asking for our help. Her husband left behind not just his loved ones. He left behind a $500,000 mortgage, credit card debt, student loans, etc. This happened 3 more times over the next year at my rotary club.

After hearing those stories I arrived at what I like to think of as an inflexion point in my career and really just how I prioritized my life. It was my personal mission to make sure that I asked every single prospect about life insurance. So, what I did was design my own jar and kept it on my desk every day. See below.

It was a great talking point that most people would always ask me about. I would explain why I have it (Rotary). It's not about guilt. It's about expressing my reason for why I am passionate about life insurance.

How many times would you have to hear this story before you took action and decided to do something? Selling is a noble profession, if we choose it to be so. For me, the last thing I want to be remembered for is my wife to be put in that position, because I did not want to buy life insurance to protect her future.

But Mike, What if I don't have a personal story/connection as to why I sell life insurance? Here are a couple of additional questions to help you craft your story:

1. Why should someone buy life insurance from you as opposed to the guy down the street?
2. What do you do really well?
3. What personal experiences do you have with life insurance?

Selling Your Product.

What's the difference between an error and a

mistake? Frequency. When I meet a financial Advisor/insurance agent the first part of my vetting process is to ask them complex financial strategy based questions. (Because, I'm a nerd, but also because I want to understand if I am in good hands.) This allows me to test someone's knowledge and overall understanding of their product. For instance, "What do you think about Indexed Universal Life Insurance or what do you think about Premium Financing?" Or asking questions about Irrevocable Life Insurance Trusts or Charitable Remainder Trusts.

Sometimes small differences make the sale. We had a couple shop us on a life insurance proposal and that happens. We pitched them a Return of Premium Term Life policy for the wife and a 10 Term with LTC for the husband. Later we found out they shopped around. Here's what happened... They went out to shop other offers. Fortunately for us the other Agency the couple spoke with had no idea what an LTC rider was. They came back the next week and signed with up. Remember your job is not to ask questions just to ask questions, remember to learn to shut up and identify when someone asks you a counter question let it sink in and actively listen. My mentor once told me, "Shut up and listen... sometimes your mouth is your biggest enemy and your ears your best friend."

But Mike, What if my product sucks?

Every product has a competitive sweet spot otherwise it wouldn't exist and you as an agent would not exist. Products and companies go through underwriting cycles called hard and soft markets. Understand what your product can do and who it fits.

Selling Your Company.

There are a lot of Agents who only sell on price and could care less about the company they sell as long as the base rate is good. These Agents are what is destroying the insurance industry. Insurance is not a commodity and if you believe it is why do you exist? Why does an Agent exist? The answer is believe it or not you provide value to the customer and insurance company. So, I ask you to decide the answer to a simple question...

You are not going to get every case approved, no matter how many carriers you represent! Get over it. The life company will not make great offers on every single case that is approved. This is why you need to find your company's 'sweet spot'. Each company has a sweet spot from a pure competitive standpoint and or a unique offering. How do you sell your company? Here are some topics to think about; Financial rating, Cash on Hand, History of AMBEST Rating, claims experience, company age, admitted vs non-admitted carriers.

But Mike, what if my company sucks?

Don't represent a bad company. It's simple. Remember perception drives action and that perception starts with your understanding of your company. So ask yourself, what does your company do well? Every company does something well, otherwise they wouldn't be selling.

"Nobody cares how much you know, until they know how much you care." - Theodore Roosevelt

Chapter 5: Objection Handling

Objection handling takes experience. There's no plug and play system for rebuttals, sometimes they work and sometimes they don't. It takes practice. Practice in your tone, your pacing, and your overall confidence in how you present your rebuttal. Don't get frustrated if someone says no. Sometimes it's not an absolute no. Sometimes it's a complaint and sometimes it's a soft no. When someone says, "I'll probably have to think about this." That's a soft objection. If someone says, "There is no way in Hell that I am buying this life policy." That might be more of an absolute no.

> *(Note) Never shut down a prospect because of an objection. An objection is generally a sign you made a mistake in your sales process and the customer has a potential un-addressed or under-addressed concern about either you, your company, or your product.*

> *(Note) Later on in the book, the reason I spend a lot of time emphasizing the needs analysis is so that you can preempt objections. If you find the right death benefit and you find the*

appropriate product for the situation, the sales process becomes an infinitely easier conversation.

(Example of Pre-Objection Handling) "Life Insurance isn't something you can just go out and buy, like a bar of soap or milk. You have to apply and qualify for a plan." What his does is set an expectation for the insured. This is an important conversation and purchase. But, not only is it an important conversation. It's an exclusive process where you have to qualify for the plan. This adds the golden rule of scarcity and exclusivity.

(Objection with signing Application) How much will this cost?

(Rebuttal): The answer is I have no idea, because someone can look perfectly healthy on the outside and might have complicated medical history on the inside. You never know.

Game Theory and Selling

Selling is a lot like playing a game of poker, because both are limited information games in a sense. The insurance company we represent sets the rules and we play the game with the prospect.

What's the 'Win Condition' with poker? You win a hand or lose a hand and it's exactly the same with selling. Either you make the sale or you do not make the sale. It's a very binary set of conditions. While we gather information about a prospect it sets us up to make better decisions during our sales process. So, ask questions and spend time qualifying each and ever prospect.

But Mike, what if they keep asking about price and rate?

As an Agent, as an advisor it's your job to steer the conversation…. Ethically. The truth is quotes in life insurance are pretty much meaningless. Most prospects have to go through stringent underwriting after you calculate a quick quote and because of that stringency you might as well wait to talk about numbers until the final presentation.

(Common Follow up Objection) You can't tell me what the premium will be?

(Rebuttal): I could give you any number. But, until we get an offer back from the life insurance company we don't know what you qualify for. Sometimes Agents will quote numbers, but if there is no medical we really have no idea. Does that make sense? This is where having conviction comes in handy because I can't tell you how many agents spew completely non-binding numbers out left and right to try to make a sale.

> *(Note) As an Agent you are an influencer not an actuary. Which is the easier conversation? The before conversation setting the expectation that we need to wait on a number and then decide how much life insurance to buy based on that rate? Or explaining an unexpected table rating or lower rating than you promised your client.*
>
> *Tip. Ever hear the saying, "If you have to ask you probably can't afford it?" Remember affordability is mostly a subject state of mind. More or less.*

(Common Objection when closing application) Do you think that's too much insurance?

(Rebuttal): Well as your insurance agent I recommend we apply for X amount just to see what the rate is, and when we get the offer back from the life insurance company, if you decide you want that amount, less than that amount, or more than amount it'll be easy to do that. You can always choose to get less after we get the offer in. Nothing is set in stone.

(Application Objection) I think I want to wait...

Few of the tactics I've learned from Agents...

1. Ask why? (Going this route really depends on how well you know the person.)
2. Or explain the process let them know an application comes with zero obligation.
3. The reason why it's important to protect your family now (sense of urgency) is that the underwriting process could take up to 3 months.

(Note) This objection needs to be handled by understanding the clients need to buy or apply along with explaining process.

(Closing Objection) I don't think I can afford that.

(Rebuttal): John, I completely understand. (Usually

pull back the application) When we first sat down you told me you need X amount of life insurance to protect your family. We've got an offer that took X amount of time to go through underwriting. As your agent I think while we have an offer in hand we should get something in place to protect your family. In a year we can re-apply to see if you can get a better rate. Sign here.

> (Note) The wording you will need to change, some Agents get afraid and try to lower the amount of insurance to justify a better 'deal'. But, remember they gave you the number for the death benefit. They need that death benefit to protect their family.

> (Add'l Note) Life insurance is a social good. Don't be pushy, but remind your client why they reached out to you in the first place. If they really can't afford it then see what they can budget. When you see the premium you can't give it context to your budget. What I mean by that is, if you can't afford something don't assume your client can't afford something.

Why is this person shopping?

Why is this person shopping for insurance? This is the heart of any good qualifying conversation. What I mean is, why now? Why didn't they buy insurance yesterday or last year or ten years ago? What is the reason for shopping? Or what is the why? People can buy life insurance from age Zero to around 85 or so. So, why then are they looking to buy at this very moment? What brings them by today?

How do I beat a cheap policy?

The short answer is beating another policy starts with you. You need to change your language, are you cheap? Do you sell cheap stuff? Someone else might, and let those agents undercut their own revenue. Be different. If you want to beat a 'cheap' policy start by attacking the amount of insurance and changing the conversation from price to value. There are three easy things you can do to 'beat' a cheap policy.

1. Offer Perm or Term with Riders
2. Focus on the amount of insurance, is it adequate?

3. Focus on a strategy, not a cost.

An easy route is to 'Don't collect $200 pass go and go straight to jail.' What I mean is if their policy is 'cheap' most often it's a term policy and you can come in as an expert with an excellent permanent insurance offering. Otherwise, you can always focus on a strategy to meet goals/needs and not a price. Price is merely the cost of value, it's the cost of protecting your family. If you want client's to get over the idea of constantly slashing insurance costs, then you need to get over it as a broker/agent.

Objection to Application. Generic objection. (Rebuttal): Not everyone qualifies for life insurance... It's kind of like applying for a job, you put in an application. You may get the job you may not, there is no guarantee. When you apply for a job are you guaranteed to get that job? Wait for answer...

> *(Note) Locking in the application is the key to selling life insurance. This is also an educational tool you should preface the entire conversation with more so than a rebuttal.*

Common Objection; I don't need life insurance, I have a policy through work.

Rebuttal Overview Abstract: Firstly, I'd always congratulation our customer on having a policy in place. Use this objection as an educational opportunity. Because, rarely is a company life insurance policy enough insurance to protect a family. First, you don't own it. It's not always portable, so if you leave the company or get fired you can't take it with you. Some group plans have portable options, make sure to check. The biggest downside to having a group plan policy is the face amount, typically face amounts are one year's salary.

Bad Press Insurance Company Objection: I've heard that your insurance company has $1,000,000,000 in unpaid death benefit. How do I know mine will be paid?

Rebuttal Overview Abstract: (Opportunity for Educating) There is a looming problem in the life insurance industry right now. Large companies have huge outstanding sums of unpaid death benefit. This is mainly due to the fact that people grow old and change phone numbers, change addresses, email addresses were not collected, agencies change, company policies forgotten about, maybe the beneficiary didn't know they were a beneficiary.

> *(Note) We had a speaker at our Rotary Club come and speak about this issue. It's a huge problem but there are emerging solutions to help find your money. She represented a company that actually would track down if you were a beneficiary with an outstanding benefit with an insurance company.*

Common Objection: "I think I need to ask my wife or spouse."

Firstly, when a prospect says this to you… how many of them end up coming back and signing up? The answer for most of us is probably a number we can count on our fingers.

Preempting Overview: The best way to avoid this objection is by having both spouses present at the initial interview and or sales presentation. Another way would be to find out beforehand if the client can make the buying decision or if they need to speak with their spouses prior to purchasing. Find out barriers to closing a sale and pre-empt them. Be transparent and present value to avoid most of these objections from coming up.

Either way try to have a face to face that involves the spouse, because it will give you the chance to insure the spouse as well. The best reason to have the non-bread winner in the loop is to show them how valuable their significant actually is. If you look at life insurance surveys most spouses wish their working spouse had more life insurance. As cold as that sounds, each spouse is more valuable than you may think.

If you summarize the L.I.F.E. with the spouse present the reactions are usually that of astonishment. Most people never actually add up the numbers or take the time to put it all together. Your biggest advocate could be the spouse who is financially dependent on the insured. Focus on the amount of insurance and the plan.

A lot of Agents will swear against doing this. For me it's an issue of transparency and respect. If you can probably bridge the gap then the outcome from my experience has been very positive. Think about it this way. If you don't address the concerns of both spouses in person, then the less agreeable/convinced spouse will address the concerns not in your presence and you can imagine where that policy goes...

If you don't do your homework to find out this answer prior to your presentation, there is really no good way to overcome, "I think I need to ask my wife." Just respect that as truth and follow up. Some people just need to talk to their spouse.

Setting the Stage

If you get one piece of good advice from this book, let it be about setting the stage. Setting expectations is direly important to executing a successful life insurance sales process. Remember to give reasons as to why you ask something. Reasons give you power and compliance science tells us it increases the likelihood a prospect agrees.

Most client objections identify weaknesses in your sales process and not setting expectations properly. The application may be easy to sell, but have you thought about selling a tough table rating? Once you've set the expectations you'll have to manage a client's expectations throughout the life insurance sales process.

Why do Client's Object?

Why do people object? Because, you haven't answered a question. Because, you haven't shown enough value. The real reason is that somewhere along your sales process they have found a chink in your armor. Every objection can be preempted and foreseen. Most people by their nature are not agreeable and most people have to say no seven times before they say yes. But, it will take you time and a lot of stumbling through presentations to master the art of objection handling.

There's a reason why one of my go to powerful questions is, "What kind of questions and concerns do you have?" The reason is that either an unanswered question and or unaddressed concern will arise in the form of an objection during closing. If we know objections are possible and readily available. Why not try flushing them out at the beginning and modify your presentation to address each concern or question?

If someone is concerned about your product, you have two choices. You can choice to be tepid and not address the customer concerns, doesn't work out great. Or you can use that concern as an opportunity to educate and solve a problem. In my experience the best way to rip off a band aide is fast. If you have bad news, head it off.

And remember a lot of objections are no more than surface level complaints and should be treated as such. People complain about prices, shocking I know! Acknowledge their concern and move on. At the end of the day we are talking about protecting someone's family here.

Preempting the Objection

Preempting objections is really as simple as setting proper expectations. Remember you are an expert and you know this process. This is why it is paramount that you explain the life insurance process to your client. For example, "Have you ever bought life insurance before?" Okay, let me take a step back and explain the process. The first step is that we do the DIME aka needs analysis and figure out how much life insurance you need...

From there we submit a non-binding application. Once the medical is done the UW process can take up to 3 months. (Seen it happen) Insert client example. It really depends on how complicated the medical history is. Once the medical is complete the life insurance will either choose to make an offer to you or reject the case (build exclusivity). But, most importantly once we have the medical complete we will know what rate you can qualify for.

Remember, most people are conditioned to say no to salespeople. The average person could object 3 times before making a buying decision as part of their buying process. It happens.

The Art of Pausing

Learning when to pause is part of the art of selling. Selling is not an exact science. You can't just have a canned statement for each situation and pause for X amount of time and get the 100% desired outcome. Each sale is different and each sale is the same. In each sale you will need to learn when not saying something becomes more valuable than saying something. Often less can be more.

Forgetting to ask Please...

When you reach into another man's fridge always ask for permission before doing so... Learn to ask to ask. Would you mind if... How does this sound so far? Would it be reasonable if we looked at... Many of you reading this have probably heard the expression, "He who talks first loses." I think this phrase should say, "If the salesman answers his own questions or is too eager to speak, he loses." Agreeableness is a trait that is very rare in society nowadays. Learn to be agreeable and it will pay huge dividends.

When you ask a question wait for an answer, even if it becomes awkward and you want to answer for the client. If the client gets the answer wrong don't correct them harshly. If you ask a specific question and the client guesses, "Well believe it or not the actual average funeral expense right now in California is around $20,000 per person."

Insurance Doctor

I've always thought doctors have the best

sales system, hands down the best system. You fill out some symptoms on a form prior to seeing the doctor. The doctor has an initial idea of what the issue is based on reading the notes from the symptom chart, but they don't rush in with a solution. They come in and you have to sit down on that weird rubber bed. The doctor reviews your symptoms, but a good doctor will ask, "What's going on?" It's a simple open ended question. You'll explain the reason for being there and remember just like a patient a prospect shows up to you for a specific reason. The doctor based on your feedback starts formulating a hypothesis as to what the problem is. If you have a good doctor, they run tests, sometimes simple and sometimes complex tests. What the doctor doesn't often do is rush to a prescription and forget to dig deeper. Once, they figure out the potential problem, they explain it and how it works. On top of that they explain options or a customized solution to the problem.

Tips to Avoid Objections / General Selling Tips

- Always be the first to agree at the onset of a conversation. Remember you are there to help not compete with the client.
- Make sure to use strategic pausing.
- Don't rush yourself or the prospect.
- Preempt the Objection with an educational piece.
- Know your Product inside and out.
- Don't be afraid of losing the sale.
- Approach selling as a conversation and collaboration.
- Have a "How can I Help?" Attitude.
- Be an authority on the subject, never stop learning.
- Read about insurance for at least 30 minutes per day.
- Dress for the occasion and client.
- Don't stray away from making eye contact.
- Use a white board to present or notepad to illustrate.
- Learn from the best in the industry and ask questions.
- Role play, role play, role play.

- Never argue with a client.
- Have standards.
- Don't judge a book by its cover.
- Try to avoid asking Yes or No Questions.

(Note) My overall mindset was simple. The prospect agreed this was the correct amount of insurance, the prospect agreed on the product, the prospect agreed on sitting down with us to explain everything, the prospect places a lot of trust in us... so what are we talking about when it comes to price? You want to think about protecting your family? Think about pinching a few pennies and placing your family at risk? What is there to think about? Don't forget. People who shop for life insurance are wildly different than people who shop for auto insurance. As Agents sometimes we forget to remember that.

As an ending note to this chapter, let me ask you a question. Do you like being sold? No. The answer is no. No one enjoys being sold a bag of goods. That being said, do you like buying things? Who doesn't love spending money? In general, if we can empower consumers to buy life insurance, it in turn will greatly reduce the time spent objection handling.

"The best revenge is massive success." - Frank Sinatra

Chapter 6: Consultative Selling, Transactional Selling and Relationship Based Selling.

What is Consultative Selling?

Consultative Selling is not all about asking more questions. It's about asking the right questions. Asking a lot of open-ended questions and following up to get some depth. How do you feel about blank? Why is that? Consultative selling is about analyzing a client's needs and designing a simple, elegant solution to meet their goals. Part of being a Trusted Advisor (consultative) is the ability to ask powerful questions. You are doing more than building a relationship, you are building value.

What is Transactional Selling?

Transactional based selling is all about selling a price and making enticements that could result in buyer's remorse. Transactional selling purely about the numbers and selling on price. Transactional selling is not a great way to approach life insurance sales, because part of the sale involves a very emotional touch point. A good example, someone calls your agency and asks for a $500,000 life insurance quote. Without thinking twice you start gathering basic underwriting information and pull up some quick quotes and spew out some completely non-binding numbers based on a preferred rating.

What is Relationship Based Selling?

Relationship based selling is based on who you know. Selling based on the relationship you built more than the product or the process. A lot of sales people fall into this category, and just so we're clear there is nothing wrong with people liking you and doing business with you because of you. But, there are only some many people that you can 'know'.

But Mike, Don't people have to like me if they want to do business with me?

Yes, but the main focal point should be your ability to help someone solve a problem and not how much they want to grab a beer with you. Don't avoid building relationships but lead with value.

What do you focus on?

Do you spend time focusing on uncontrollable events/variables? Do you spend your time focusing on abundance or worrying about scarcity? Do you focus on having a plan and executing strategies? The reason I wanted to bring up focus, is that because focus can make or break a salesperson.

Here's an example of what a Transactional Sales Agent focuses on, the rate, gossip, and any other uncontrollable event that comes up in the course of an Agent's day. "Selling insurance is all about the rate." "The rate is all that matters." Ever hear this nonsense coming from some agents? "We're not competitive..." So why do some agents thrive an others fail? It's an Agent's mentality. A Consultative Trusted Advisor focuses on the client's needs, keeps a focus on ways to build/present value, learns/presents new techniques, focuses on perfecting systems, and protecting assets/families.

What can you control in the Life Insurance Sales Process? Can you control the rate? No. Can you control how prepared you are? Yes. Can you control having a process? Yes. Can you control your product design? Yes. Forget about what you cannot control.

Consultative Strategies

The two prominent approaches I've used in the past revolve around fulfilling a need for your client or solving a problem for your client. A Trusted Advisor should be able to walk a client through multiple scenarios and product details. Be able to handle almost any product question, from experience and from preparation.

Consultative strategies involve a lot of preparation and fact finding. Fact finding and knowing when to listen are key to effective consultative strategy execution. But, you also have to know how to leverage those facts and be creative. Remember, you were given one mouth and two ears. Use this ratio accordingly when communicating. People want to be asked questions not barked at with insurance factoids and lingo.

Transactional Strategies

A typical Transactional Sales Strategy revolves around Selling the Rate or Selling a Product. Transactional strategies are usually based on 'shopping' the market or some other price gauging strategy.

Most Transactional Agents will complain about rates and say their Insurance Company is not competitive, pay them no mind. Another example of transactional selling would be selling a life insurance policy to get an auto discount. What value does a discount provide? In my opinion a discount provides little to no value. Discounts and savings are not the primary concern for a person buying life insurance. The primary driver should always be the need to protect their family or assets.

A life product provides benefits and the benefits should justify the price. If you cheapen an item the focus becomes on the price and you instantly commoditize the life policy. If you provide a valuable service and a product, the price should stand by itself.

Ending Note

Do you want to solve problems or create problems? Do you want to provide solutions or have someone provide solutions to your client? If all you do is sell term insurance on price, you'll end up creating all your own challenges in the long term. Think about it for a second. What happens if your client becomes uninsurable upon the expiration of the term? What happens if the face amount of the policy isn't enough over time? What is the insured becomes disabled and cannot pay premiums? What if they require long term care?

You can't build a reputation on what you are going to do. – Henry Ford

Chapter 7: Other Considerations

Replacement Life Policy Strategies

Replacing a life insurance policy can be highly risky and is typically not a great way to sell life insurance. Replacing existing policies opens the Agent up to potentially large Errors and Omissions exposures as well. Ask yourself and hopefully the insured why they want to replace the policy before eagerly re-writing the policy. Is it for price? Is it to be with your agency? Is it because the company?

The problem with replacing a policy, is that you are enticing a client to surrender a current life insurance policy for another with you. They may lose key benefits that previous policy had attached to it, such as cash value, insurability rights, age lock-ins, rating, etc. Personally, I was never comfortable enough to switch policies, but it's up to you.

But Mike, What if my client has a bad policy?

Use your best judgment. But remember it's always a risk you take when cancelling an existing policy. At the end of the day you are liable for any errors in judgment.

401K vs IUL/VUL: Comparing Insurance to Investment Accounts

Another risky selling strategy is asset re-allocation. Some Agents try to divert funds from 401(K) or IRA contributions into life insurance products. I would recommend NEVER doing this. I've seen sales presentations where a qualified plan is being compared to an IUL or VUL.

As a rule of thumb I don't compare an after tax life insurance product to a qualified plan. Qualified plans are not life insurance and life insurance products are not retirement plans. Life Insurance is meant for someone with a life insurance need. Life insurance shouldn't be used as a sole retirement plan.

Life Insurance Retirement Plan

One of the oldest permanent life insurance strategies is called the L.I.R.P. Short for a Life Insurance Retirement Plan. Typically these plans are funded with a Variable or Indexed Universal Life Plan. The L.I.R.P can be funded with just about any Permanent Policy, but depending on the policy it can make a huge difference with the illustration and outcome.

Let's use Indexed Universal Life as an example. Indexed Universal Life Plans can be great supplemental retirement plans in theory. Here's how it works. You buy two things. You buy life insurance in the event you pass away. You also buy a savings account that can earn up to x% interest over time. The savings account is what builds your cash value. In this savings account your money is invested with a management fee and can earn up to x%. How is it a retirement plan? The money you are putting into the 'savings-like account' can one day be taken out tax free as a loan.

But Mike, that sounds too good to be true…

Time will tell. But, yes for the most part it is. The industry has been all over the place since the inception of the IUL and VUL. I'm using the word savings account very loosely because there are no FDIC protections built into safeguard the money and the money is no easily accessible without MANY conditions.

In simple terms. The LIRP requires you pay

$100 a month in premium. $50 goes toward paying for the life insurance and $50 into the 'savings-like account'. Over time the interest in theory will grow your cash value and you can take a loan against the cash value.

Remember for a LIRP to be successful it should only work as a supplemental retirement plan and be overfunded to get the maximum benefit with an increasing death benefit. Overfunding involves paying higher premiums than the target premium, but below the Modified Endowment Contract levels.

The benefit of a LIRP is simple. Currently the government has allowed Cash Value in Life Insurance policies to be loaned against and not taxed as income, because it's a loan not income. As long as a minimum amount of premium remains being contributed and cash value of the policy remains above a certain specified level, the policy loan remains untaxed.

A LIRP can be a powerful consultative strategy for clients who like Dollar Cost Averaging and the idea of never losing principal. Also, the beauty of an IUL or VUL is that there is a tax free death benefit. A

L.I.R.P can also be a great supplement plan for clients who have a hard time saving consistently and doesn't want to actively invest.

But Mike, this sounds too good to be true, what's the catch?

See below.

Downfalls of Indexed Universal Life Insurance.
1. Policy Loans have no guaranteed interest rate. Meaning that when you take your money out you don't know what the interest rate on your loan will be. It's completely up to the life insurance company who will be holding your money hostage.
2. Cost of Insurance will most likely increase each year requiring the client to put in more money each year or take less investment gains. It's completely up to the life insurance company who will be holding your money hostage.
3. The Rate Cap or ceiling for investment income is not guaranteed either. So, when you buy the policy the ceiling can be 10% and the next year can be 5%. It's

completely up to the life insurance company who will be holding your money hostage.
4. You are required to pay a 1% management fee. If the S&P 500 which is the most popular way your money is investment tanks and loses 50% you lose nothing because you have a floor of 0%, but you still have to pay a management fee of 1% at least.
5. There are no Federal protections on your cash value.
6. If you take too much money out in the loan you can end up paying taxes due to what is called a Modified Endowment Contract.
7. There is normally a 10 year minimum break-even point, conservatively. So, if you want your money within now and 10 years you are S.O.L.

Pension Maximization

Pension Maximization is an interesting concept. This strategy is very straight forward. A person who is eligible for a pension normally has three options normally to take as a payout.

First, they can take all the money in cash.

Second they can choose to take the money based on their life expectancy. Third they can take the money based on their life expectancy and their spouses. The first and third option result in lower long term payouts per installment. Let's use the second option. A man who is 55 retires from his company and lives ten years receiving $50,000 per year for ten years or $500,000. And now his family has nothing.

In the third option, which most people tend to choose. The man retires at 55 and lives 10 years with a $35,000 payout option. The wife who typically will live longer lives another 10 years after that still drawing the $35,000. In total at ager 65 they made a combined $700,000.

Just to recap.

- Option one $4000 per month.
- Option two $3000 per month.

Pension Maximization is an easy concept, invest the difference in a permanent life insurance plan.

So. If you would have been living off of the $3000 a month anyways that gives you an extra $1000 a month to put into a life insurance plan. If the man outlives his life expectancy, great he can take a loan against his cash value. If he dies the spouse receives a huge death benefit, which would have paid out more than the pension because the death benefit is tax free and up front. You can even annuitize the death benefit to outpace the monthly payments the spouse would have been receiving compared to the second to die pension payout.

How do you talk about you?

If someone meets you at a networking event, when they go home, how do they describe what you do to their spouse?

- A Trusted Advisor, "I help clients protect their families and assets by providing financial guidance through providing consultative life insurance strategies."
- A Sales Agent, "I sell life insurance."

Selling on Value vs Selling on Price.

Price is a surface level concern like an iceberg you may just see a small portion of a person's concern. When you take a consultative selling approach you have to dig deeper. When someone tells you something is too expensive, you merely have not successfully convinced/demonstrated them of the value. Or if they say that's a lot of money. Just agree. It is but we are talking about protecting your client's family!!! Do you provide value? Do you provide a valuable service? Do you care about people? Do you learn any more or do think you've learned all there is?

You have to ask yourself what purpose you serve as an agent. For me it was being a trusted advisor who could answer almost any insurance question or find the answer, analyze needs and goals while providing a simple solution in plain language. I realized very early on that I wouldn't close every sale, so I crafted my strategy around educating, making a practical recommendations with me or with someone else, and focused on protecting assets and families.

We tend especially now with so much online competition and multi company rating platforms that insurance is about buying peace of mind and the price for that is the premium. Not all insurance is created equal and customers care about more than price. Some customers care about price as a sole factor for making a determination. Most people take price into consideration when buying insurance. But, that doesn't always have to be the main focus of the conversation nor should it be.

If you want to be a trusted advisor you need to ask meaningful questions. Figure out what your client cares about. I've had clients who were passionately driven to build a charity or build an endowment for a charity. Asking meaningful questions serves an important part in the overall process, it helps you uncover those deeper concerns (other than price) and find what people truly value.

I can't stress this point enough. Price is a surface level concern, because it has no context. Price is only an objection when value hasn't been demonstrated to justify it. People make purchases all the time they can't afford, why do you think credit cards are so popular? If it's important enough to a person they will find a way. Now of course there is a limit to this mentality. A good rule of thumb most advisors use, is that a person should invest 10% of his income on life insurance.

But Mike, What if my policies keep cancelling?

Having trouble with chargebacks (clients cancelling within the 1st year)? We all get chargebacks and some will be unexpected. If it becomes a persistent problem in your agency or your business, look at the source. Sometimes we oversold a concept or didn't garner stakeholder feedback (asking spouse). What often happens is we tend to sell the maximum amount of insurance as many times as possible to maximize our commission, it happens. But, the unintended consequence of this can be that the person really couldn't afford what we sold them and they ended up shopping us once the bills started stacking up. Also, look at your follow up process. How often do you follow up? Do clients tend to habitually cancel around the same time? If so, what does that tell you about needed follow up?

How do I get a referral partner to reciprocate?

This a question I get all the time. We all have attempted to set up referral arrangements where we play that awkward game of 'who will give the first lead out.' It's the business way of playing 'chicken'. So, what do you do? There is no one size fits all answer. The answer I think makes the most sense is to set proper expectations. Know what you're getting into before you get into it.

Part 3: Sales Process

"I read, I study, I examine, I listen, I think, and out of all that I try to form an idea into which I put as much common sense as I can." - Marquis de Lafayette

Chapter 8: Prospecting / Active Marketing Plans

Remember in the movie Ground Hog Day when Bill Murray is approached by his long lost high school classmate who now happens to be a Life Insurance Agent? If you don't go back and re-watch it. When prospecting remember a great way to have people running for the hills is to start out talking about how you sell life insurance and the wonders of the indexed universal life insurance policy.

Prospecting is the lifeblood of your agency and for that matter your pocket book. Work hard until you can work smart. The most effective Agents are constantly prospecting for new clients, especially if you sell life only. A lot of Agents neglect prospecting. Prospecting for life insurance to be frank is much more laborious work than selling life insurance. Selling Life Insurance is easy... You figure out how to identify a client's life benefit need, you learn your product, and you set a process in place and repeat.

My prospecting method was simple, to have at least 7 active marketing activities in my marketing plan. I would allow each activity to run for a year and track the progress. If during that year my results were not producing enough, I would make adjustments.

What is prospecting?

What did prospectors do during the gold rush? They sat by the river beds and sifted through dirt. But, in their process of sifting through dirt, eventually they would uncover and discover golden nuggets. In insurance the old adage sticks, prospecting comes down to talking to enough people and saying the right things.

Just remember when you use these techniques. It doesn't have to be a checklist. It's more of a guide to get people talking. What I found early on in my career was that everyone has a favorite subject, themselves. And if you don't know how to be interesting start by becoming interested. People love to talk about themselves.

But Mike, I'm not interesting and I have a hard time meeting people in networking groups...

If you don't know how to be interesting start by becoming interested. Most people like to talk about themselves and their interests. From a prospecting standpoint I've always found it effective to ask about occupation, family, friends and enjoyment. Start by asking questions and you will find people tend to open up quite easily. Remember you are not interrogating someone but these questions might help you start become interested.

1. What do you do for a living? (Occupation or Activity)
2. How long have you been doing it for?
3. Do you like it? What do you like about it?
4. How did you get involved in that?
5. What do you do really well? (Occupationally)

Ideas for Marketing Activities

With marketing act ivies or prospecting activities remember that what you do usually produces who you speak with. So keep in mind your brand. What is congruent with your agency? Which customers are the customers that you can help and want to be future clients?

Cross Selling (If mutli-line agent) - I wanted to

start this list with the lowest of low hanging fruit. If you are a multi-line agency, you have clients who may only have an auto or home policy and have a need life insurance.

Upselling clients with small company policies. - If you have clients with small non-portable life policies, explain the difference. It's like renting, you don't own a company policy. If that company goes out of business or you leave the company you leave your life insurance.

Referral Partnerships - Attorneys, Real Estate, Mortgage Officers, Accountants, Stock Brokers, Funeral Homes, P&C Agents, Health or Benefits only Agents, Commercial Real Estate brokers, Financial Advisors, etc.

Chamber of Commerce - The Chamber of Commerce is such a reliable source of income, if you spend the time to work it. A good chamber of commerce is like gold for an insurance Agent.

Cold Calling - Cold Calling is a close to extinct form of marketing. Not only is it inefficient, the effectiveness is questionable at best for life insurance. With the new TCPA cold calling has been greatly diminished as a marketing source. It may work for some people, but it's very taxing.

Door Knocking – Door knocking houses can be tough, but businesses on the other hand can be a gold mine. Most business owners are still an underserved community of people who need life insurance.

Mailer follow ups - The largest life insurance policy to date $200,000,000 face amount was sold from a mailer in Santa Barbara California. We ran a highly successful mailer campaign in an affluent area. We sent post cards into a 7 and 8 figure neighborhood and picked up a client worth around $80,000,000 to $100,000,000.

Social Media Marketing - Social Media can be a great use of your time if done correctly. There are substantial compliance issues to consider. It's best to speak with you securities principal about marketing activities beforehand.

Radio or Podcasting - I'm friends with a Realtor who has a Saturday afternoon AM Real Estate radio program that is becoming wildly successful. He answers real estate related questions and generates prospects from the show.

Affiliations - A friend of mine is a life insurance broker who served in the Navy for 22 years and he was able to generate a substantial amount business from the Navy. What kind of affiliations do you have?

Client Referrals – Client referrals are a great way to create a rich flow of high quality leads. Some Agents prefer asking for referrals at the time of the application signing. Some Agents prefer to ask for referrals at the time of policy delivery. The key to getting client referrals is consistently asking, just ask.

Charitable Boards – Charitable boards offer great exposure to advanced market prospects. The one downside is being on a board gives you possible D&O exposure. Sitting on boards gives you a high level overview of the organization but also allows you to get very involved on the charitable side.

Community Events – One of my go to events was a local small classic car show on the weekend in my hometown. I started off by sponsoring the car show by providing doughnuts.

Associations and Groups - Networking groups and social clubs are great ways to prospect. People like to do business with people they have things in common with. What do you do on the weekend? I watch a lot of fights and golf. So, I'm friends with a lot of people who like to watch fights and golf.

Lunch and Learn or Fish Bowl– Lunch and Learns are powerful ways to drive new business and it allows you to collaborate with other experts in complimentary fields. Having a recurring fish bowl at a restaurant is still an effective way to drum up business.

Business Owners Life Policies – One highly underserved market to this day is business owners and prospecting business owners can be a highly effective way to develop your practice. This also opens up more permanent strategies for you as well.

Buying Life Leads – Buying life insurance leads is extremely profitable. But, it comes with a certain level of frustration knowing that some of the information is fraudulent or fakery. Most successful agents buy insurance leads. It's not for everyone and has a large commitment of investment capital.

Life Insurance Triggering Events

What is a trigger event? It's a life event that should 'trigger' you to re-evaluate their life insurance needs. Does your client fall into one of these events?

1. Recently had a child?
2. Having a child?
3. Had a child move back home?
4. Had a recent auto accident?
5. Had a home claim?
6. Will be getting married?
7. Thinking about changing jobs?
8. Losing a job?
9. Getting a promotion?
10. Is your client renting?
11. Buying a new car?
12. Refinancing their home?

What do you know about the big life events coming up in your client's life? As your client gets older they will experience events which make them need life insurance or at least need to evaluate their needs for life insurance. Remember at different life stages people will have events in their life that trigger a possible need for life insurance or at the very least a review.

Transitioning Statements

Transitions have to fit your process, fit your client's life cycle and fit the triggering event. Transitioning will be different for everyone and each situation. But, for beginners stick to the same transition and see what plays well with folks you speak with. You don't want to box a client in with a statement and force a yes or no answer. We want them to think. By asking the following question with an assumptive tone if the client says, "I don't have life insurance." Then you can usually see some distress as a normal person a person in their situation should have some in place by my question.

The easiest transition for me was, "By the way who do you have your life insurance with?" Transitioning is best done with a question that requires some introspection. For example, "Now we have insured your car and protected your home... What's protecting your family if you become ill or something happens?" Start with these industry common transitions to become consistent and eventually you can design a transition that goes with your flow.

General Rapport Building Advice

Building rapport is much like building the foundation of a house. You could lay your foundation and right after the inspectors leave pull the rebar from the cement. Or you could build everything to code and make a strong lasting foundation. Either way you can build a home.

People tend to make judgments in the first two seconds of an initial meeting. Scientists tell us that we have less than 7 seconds to make a good first impression. Making a good first impression isn't easy, because most people just don't know how to be interesting. So, if you don't know how to be interesting do the next best thing. Be interested.

Life Insurance can be done face to face or from a distance. From sales education we know that face to face sales in life insurance generally results in a higher closing ratio. But, again what will increase your odds?

If you decide to go the face to face route there are a few considerations. How you decide to dress and present yourself will make a huge amount of difference in the sale. How you make eye contact will make a huge difference. How you shake someone's hand will make a huge difference.

"I hated every minute of training, but I said, 'Don't quit. Suffer now and live the rest of your life as a champion.'" – Muhammad Ali

Chapter 9: The First Presentation (Define the Benefit/Product and Submit Application)

The first presentation is simple. You have a strong opening, determine a death benefit, find a product to fulfill the need, get a commitment to submit an application and then get a commitment to get a conditional receipt of insurance.

Here is the process:

1. Opening Statement
2. Needs Analysis and Qualifying
3. Determine A Death Benefit
4. Product Design
5. Submit the Application
6. Close the App and get Conditional Insurance

But Mike, How do I make a persuasive presentation?

It all starts with structure and then filling in the pieces. The key to a great presentation is to get the prospect engaged by asking those questions we spoke about earlier. Get them engaged and pull out concerns they have. Pull out personal anecdotes they might have about insurance or possible questions.

A life insurance sales presentation is easy. The life insurance sales process is an interplay of setting and managing expectations, educating, and finding a product that fits a client's needs analysis.

Opening questions

Most sales books emphasis closing techniques. Opening is much more important that closing. Your opening sets the stage for your entire presentation. Your opening sets the pace for the sales process. The best way to open is with an interesting question or an interesting topic of discussion.

What's the powerful question you can start a consultative conversation with? In my opinion, "How can we help?" Most book emphasis closing techniques. In my opinion both the opening and the close are equally as important. It's simple, it's elegant, and it has a way of disarming a prospect who could be nervous about a touchy subject. What powerful questions do you use during your opening presentation?

- "What kind of specific questions and concerns do you have?"

- "John, why are you looking for life insurance?"
- "Have you purchased life insurance before? What was the experience like?"
- "How can we help?"
- "How fast did you want to start protecting your family, today or tomorrow?"
- "Assuming we could find you the plan that fit your budget, was enough to protect your family and with the right insurance company, would you want the policy to start immediately?"

The opening is also where you explain the, "You, Your Process/Product and Your Company." Remember people do business with sales people that they know, like and trust. It's really important that your opening questions do not talk about product. Opening questions are meant to discover intent to buy, reasons for buying, and why they came to you.

But Mike, How do I Determine a client's Death Benefit?

A client calls you on the phone and asks you to quickly quote a $500,000 term life insurance policy?

So, eager to close a policy your instinct is to rattle out some numbers that are in no way guaranteed or binding.

Based on your age it comes out to blah blah blah a month as you sit back and wait for his/her routing number. The client thanks you and then shoots the breeze for a bit before hanging up. You sit at your phone looking confused as to why they didn't immediately want to sign up. Has this happened before? Happened to me before. Now I know better.

The fundamental mistake most agents make when they are new is that they don't ask. They don't ask why, they don't ask how, they don't inquire and they do not investigate. Sometimes when a case seems like a softball it still requires a detailed approach even though it may seem someone is ready to buy immediately. Sometimes the exact opposite can happen. This requires experience to determine when people put out buying signal or put out signals of inquiry. Most people see those $5 per month term policies advertised on television and then call you wondering if that is the case. It usually takes a bit of investigation to figure out why they are looking and how they arrived at that specific amount.

What are the simplest ways to determine a client's death benefit? Here are a couple I used in the past:

1. L.I.F.E – Loans, Income, Funeral Cost, Education = Death Benefit.
2. Needs Based Approach – immediate and future expenses.
3. Human Life Value Approach – Income earning potential with growth.
4. Simple – Savings, Income, Mortgage, Pension, Loans, Education / Expenses = Death Benefit.

(Note) When determining the income portion of life insurance a good rule of thumb is to at least cover 5 years up to 10 years. The key is to use a system and be consistent. Any of these systems work for either permanent or term insurance.

(Remember) Client's don't have vast life insurance knowledge most of the time, keep it simple and keep the client in mind. Your job is to educate not barrage them with your

knowledge and slap them across the face with your Series Licenses. Also, these systems will allow you with little ease to determine a person's disposable income, for budgetary purposes.

But Mike, Why these systems?

These systems will keep you consistent. How do you know if something works if you don't consistently use it? Get out of your own way and don't try to reinvent the wheel. These systems are time tested and have been used for decades. Develop your own system over time or right out of the gate but stick to a system. Make your own system that works with your overall flow. Just have a system that you can use earnestly each time you sell life insurance or determine a benefit.

(Note) It's important that as an advisor the client ultimately is responsible for coming up with the numbers. The death benefit is their number determined by their numbers.

L.I.F.E – The life conversation is a simple way to determine a client's death benefit.

Usually I start the conversation by asking,

"Jon, how much life insurance do you think you need, or were you looking for some guidance?" At this point people will most likely do one of two things.

- Throw out a big round number
- Ask for some guidance

Most clients don't know how much life insurance they need or want or what makes sense. So this question usually gets the desired answer. Most people say, "I'd like some guidance." If they on the off chance say I need $500,000 of life insurance that is even easier. Because, it allows you to ask, "Okay, great. How did you arrive at that number?"

From that point, it's an easy process. "We have an easy way to determine how much life insurance you need to protect your family." And it goes like this, "We use a formula called L.I.F.E. to figure out how much we need." Walk through the formula. "Loans, Income, Funeral Expenses, Education."

Asking someone how much debt is as easy as a conversation as you make it. If you make it awkward it will be awkward. If you make it comfortable it will be comfortable. If you make it uncomfortable, it will be. Remember a sale is a lot like a play, people who haven't seen the play don't realize you've messed up until you let them know.

"Do you own your home or rent?" If so, "How much do you have left on the mortgage?" "Just a ballpark." Explore a little more, "Any other debt, like credit card or cars..." Wait for an answer. If you develop decent rapport then people will be fairly forthcoming with the information and bring it up without you prying too much.

Income, "How many years of income do you want to replace?" Again put the onus on the client to make a decision so you don't force an answer on them. If it's uncomfortable for you to ask someone how much money they make, just think of it like a band-aide. Do you pull it off quick or slow? Either way it gets pulled off, just ask. This also allows you to ask, "Did you want to replace income until the kids are out of college?"

"Roughly, how much would you say your income per year is before taxes?" Experts vary about how many years may be appropriate for replacing income. Leave it up to the client or provide some guidance. "How many years would you like to replace your income?" As a rule of thumb I would recommend anywhere from 5 to 20 depending on the situation.

Funeral Expenses, "If you were to guess, what you think funeral costs run these days?" The reason I like to ask this question is the fact most people have had to deal with this cost at some point and have a personal reference they bring up. "That's right, it's around $20,000!"

Education. Education makes the man (or woman). I'd always steal that line from Shawshank when Andy asks the guard, "Would you rather your kids go to Harvard or Yale?" But, sometimes people have education expenses and college debt top of mind. It's an easy opener for someone to latch on to.

So, now we have established the costs and outstanding expenses associated with someone passing away. The method is simple and may be too simple for certain situations. As a rule of thumb either of these two methods accomplishes establishing a rough estimation of Death Benefit needs.

After calculating the Death Benefit it's time to present it. At this point I would normally just ask, "So, based on your numbers it looks like you would need to apply for approx., $744,304 in insurance. Do you feel like that is enough insurance to protect your family?"

Personal Balance Sheet Approach

The Personal Balance Sheet Approach is a combination approach I came up with that combines aspects of the Human Life Value approach and the Needs Approach along with L.I.F.E. It flushes out the amount of assets a person has and the liabilities. It also gives you a clear idea of what the person has in the bank and can budget.

How many of your clients have a 401K? How many have savings? How many have stored away assets of some kind big or small? This approach is quite detailed, but it allows you to get insights into your client's financial health. What this allows you to do is understand what the person's actual budget is and how to leverage life insurance.

The first time we set up a charitable life insurance plan we did so by understand where our client was spending their money. We ran into a budgeting objection and then realized that the client was tithing 15% of his income to the church. So, after explaining how we could re-allocate some of that to buy a life policy it made it an easy sale. Half of the benefit went to church and half to the family of the client, protecting both the church if it lost a donor and the family if it lost the bread winner.

(Note) This approach isn't for newbies. You have to be confident enough to dig deep into a prospects financial situation.

Needs Analysis and Qualifying Process

What questions do you ask a client during your presentation? Why do you ask those questions? Which order do you ask those questions? If you look at your qualifying process as a Thanksgiving dinner, what would the center piece be? A simple question, does this person need life insurance?

If you truly want to be a consultative agent, you have to have standards. Having standards means you stand for something. Sounds redundant, I know. But, you have to know which clients will be suited for your agency and which clients can be better served elsewhere. The biggest mistake I made when opening, was the idea that I could be an agent for every insurance need. Remember the carriers you represent will have a sweet spot for each line of insurance, it's your job to find it.

When you think carrier appetite and competitive sweet spot, what do you think of? How well do you know the company you represent? Where does your company play? Some companies offer Heart Rate monitors and weight loss programs as incentives to drive down underwriting costs.

But Mike, my company is just not competitive on price...

When you qualify a prospect you need to understand what your company can and can't do well. It's equally important to understand what your company can not do well.

Can your company offer table shavings? Can your company offer non-medical underwriting for permanent policies? Does your company have a hyper competitive sweet spot for Term policies under the age or 18? Does your company focus on conversion term plans? Does your company allow re-writes for term policies with the same medical rating as the policy you are re-writing? Does your company write marijuana smokers as non-smokers? Does your company write tobacco chewers as non-smokers?

But Mike, Shouldn't I ask about the Person's budget for life insurance?

Asking a person about their budget for life insurance is about as useless as a person asking about a quote for life insurance. The truth is a budget is more or less subjective. People buy things that go over their budget all the time. That's why we have credit cards. The process I use relies a lot of deductive reasoning. If I know a person's income and expenses I can generally understand what they can "afford." That's why you have to learn to invoke emotions into the conversation. If you make it a mechanical transactional sale then it's easy for the customer to say no.

Other Qualifying Questions

Why are they buying? Have they tried in the

past to get life insurance? Who will their beneficiary be? Why did they choose that beneficiary? Are there lawyer or accountant viewed as a trusted advisor? Don't be afraid to dig deep into a client's financial position. Use your best judgment on a case by case basis.

As you learn more about a prospective client you can determine whether or not they are a 'right fit' for your agency. Remember as an Agent you are a field underwriter and should know who makes a good fit for your insurance company and for your agency. Pre-qualifying is a key part of your sales process, it'll save you time and frustration.

Building a Qualifying Process

Build a process for qualifying is paramount to your success. Everything you need and want to know about a client to help them achieve their goals. With life insurance a client could have many goals, so building a qualifying process should have both general and specific questions. Look to your carrier to see what current material they may have, most companies offer qualifying workflows or needs analysis templates. L.I.F.E might be too simplistic for most of your permanent cases, but for term it's an easy starting off point.

Product Selection.

At this point we have uncovered and discovered why the prospect needs to buy life insurance. We have determined the amount of life insurance using the prospect's own numbers and our system. Now we have to determine which product fulfills the need. So, how do we do that? It's going to depend a lot on income, the death benefit and how the person feels about insurance. For the purposes of this book we are going to focus mostly on term insurance.

Farmer Analogy and Bucket Strategy

If you plan on pitching a blended or permanent product try using this analogy some time. The bucket strategy is fairly common and simple to execute for permanent policies. There are three types of retirement buckets; currently taxable, deferred taxable income, and never taxed. Do you want to be taxed now, later, or never? There are only two options that fall into the never taxed bucket. Life Insurance (assuming it doesn't MEC) and College Savings Plans.

A great analogy for this strategy is the Farmer analogy. If you were a Farmer would you rather pay taxes on the seed or pay taxes on the crop? If you pay on the seed your crop won't grow to its full potential.

Or how would you like to not pay taxes on the crop at all? It's a good lead in to talk about the tax free status of life insurance loans. Figure out an easy way to relate life insurance to your customers. Coming up with analogies will save you countless headaches.

Estate Planning Opener Advanced Markets, "So, you've accumulated all of this massive wealth, how much of it would you like to go to the government and how much would you like to go to your heirs?" Work with an estate planner and your TPA to develop easy transitions, openers, and compliant scripts

Sell the Medical Exam.

Let's assume at this point we have determined the death benefit and determined the client wants temporary insurance or permanent insurance and you have explained the product in simple terms. So now you sell the Medical Exam.

Me: "So, the next step in the process is that we submit the application and set up the Medical Exam. There's no money needed unless you wanted conditional insurance."

Client: "What is conditional insurance?" Everyone asks unless they have had a recent policy issued.

Tip: The reason I bring up conditional insurance every time is twofold, one it's important and two it helps build value (as most agents neglect to explain it at all).

Me: "Glad you asked. As we discussed before it could take up to 3 months to get an offer from the life company. Hopefully we get something in two weeks, but it happens sometimes. Conditional insurance would cover you during that time period." Pause.

Client: "What do we need to set that up?"

Me: "It's pretty easy. All we would need is

about one month of estimated premium." Wait for response. If yes, set it up. If no, note they rejected it.

Me: "So, here's what we are going to do. Let's set up a time for nurse to come out to your house or business for the medical. Would you rather have them come to your house or business?"

I go through a checklist in my educational sales process:

1. The client chose the death benefit with their math, and our help.
2. The client chooses the type of life insurance, with our help.
3. The client chooses the endorsements, with our help.
4. The client chooses if they want conditional insurance or not, with our help.
5. The client chooses where and when the Para Med is completed.

Getting a commitment to get the Medical Exam/application/conditional receipt done through your agency shows a lot of trust. Usually, it reduces the chance the client goes and shops. I don't bring up price except in the case of conditional insurance. I can't stress this enough, I tried to never put a number in our client's mind. Or at least never make the number a focus, because if we bought conditional insurance we would have to figure out a rough premium to estimate the down payment.

Because, it's near impossible to recover from when the offer comes back wildly higher than the quote. It's obviously your discretion, because I'm not a consultant or your boss. But, it's a tough unnecessary conversation in my opinion that can be easily avoided with the proper consultative preempted conversations.

Ask for the sale. Don't be afraid. So, here's what we're going to do. Let's set up a medical exam. It's a simple process where we have a nurse come out and do a brief medical exam. They can come to your home or work. Which do you prefer?

But Mike, if I don't give them a quote how do I know how much to put down for the down payment on the conditional insurance?

Just use 10% of the estimated premium or a single month's estimated premium.

Good, Better and Best: The Red Herring of Sales

When I first started in the insurance industry a lot of Agents were still clinging onto the Good, Better and best sales presentation. With life insurance keep it simple. The more options you give someone the more opportunity you give them to back out of the sale or go shop you. Remember you are the trusted advisor. Once you have determined the correct amount of insurance and the correct product/company... advise your client! The easiest way to learn how to sell insurance is by focusing on selling the medical exam not the rate.

How do I know when to present Perm over Term?

A lot of Agents have a hard time knowing when to offer permanent insurance over term insurance. The answer is... it depends on the client. The easiest way is to ask your prospect. Have a brief teaser presentation and use it as a barometer for each client. The key to explaining permanent insurance is to simply explain cash value accumulation and the tax free status of policy loans. But, remember you need to develop something that goes with the flow of your presentation. As you start qualifying and fact finding you should have a relatively easy time figuring this out.

Some questions to ponder:
- When is the time horizon for insurance?
- Do they have lot's of disposable income and high tax liability?
- Do they not have a financial plan?
- Do they have a defined benefit pension plan?
- Do they have assets?
- Are they asking buying questions? Or expressing interest?

But Mike, how do I know when I'm in rapport with a client?

What I like to do is matching and mirroring. Early on in the presentation if you are sitting across from a prospect start by matching their posture. If you lean in do they lean back or in? If you lean back does the prospect take a more relaxed posture as well? And it's funny throughout the presentation if someone is agreeable and in sync with your presentation they tend to mirror the movements you make. If someone crosses their arms it usually indicates a barrier, or sometimes it just shows they are cold.

Think of selling like poker. Poker is classified as a limited information game. The client usually has two pieces of info or two cards. They know how much they want to pay or some assumption of price based on a television ad and they have an idea of coverage. As you begin to qualify you begin to gather information and that information if used correctly will help you play your hand so to speak. What does this client care about besides price? What is this client looking to insure? What is this life policy protecting? Flushing out the emotion makes your 'implied odds' of closing a sale go up. This allows you also to further customize your offering and helps the client make a better more well informed decision, just like in poker. Each hand you have implied odds at beating the other player. The more card on the table the more information. The more tells the other person has the more information you get to make your decision. Empower the consumer with information by asking questions and leveraging those answers into solutions you can provide.

Closing Questions

There are thousands of closing questions and techniques. I would recommend reading any book by Grant Cardone to learn some new closes. My go to with every single life sale was, "How would you like to pay?" It doesn't work for everyone. But, I kept it simple and it would throw most people off with how simple it was.

As a Consultative Agent or Trusted Advisor, your closing questions should be powerful and precise. Don't shy away from asking the client for the sale. If you have presented value it should be an easy Segway into signing the documentation and getting your client on the road to being protected.

The richest person in the world is the perennial student. – Michael Bonilla

Chapter 10: The Last Presentation: Presenting the offer from the insurance company.

The last presentation is the easiest part of the sales process. Remember life insurance is a front loaded sales process. At this point it could be anywhere from 1 week to 3 months from the point at which you submitted the application. Let's recall what you have done to this point.

1. Flushed out any possible questions/concerns the prospect has.
2. Taken the time to sit down face to face. (ideally)
3. Explained the value added service you provide.
4. Determined the death benefit using the client's numbers.
5. Determined a suitable product to meet that need.
6. Explained how the insurance works.
7. Obtained a signed application.
8. Obtained conditional insurance. (ideally)
9. Set up and completed a Medical Exam.

10. Received Approval from underwriting and received a rating.

That's right. You did all of that just to sell a life insurance policy. There has been a tremendous amount of 'buy-in' by the prospect all ready. So, now is time to present the offer. Remember to be consistent with the modality in which you present. Not every sale has to be over the phone, or in person or by email. But, be consistent and congruent with your presentation style.

When you present the offer just simply recap the amount of insurance the prospect applied for and why that was important to them in their own words. Recap the product design and point out anything pertinent the prospect should know before purchasing.

(Note) This conversation is not meant to be lengthy. You've done a tremendous amount of work up until this point from prospecting, to the needs analysis, to filling out an application, to underwriting, to receiving an offer...

"Hi Bob, We have great news! The life insurance company has made an offer. XYZ Insurance Company is willing to make you an offer for the full amount we applied for, which is great. We also got an incredible rate XYZ premium per month." And then shut up.

> *(Note) The reason we emphasis the rate here is not to sell based on the rate. Up until this point price was never a focal point of the discussion (unless permanent strategy). The reason I would always prefer talking about monthly premiums is the fact that monthly numbers are just easier to digest. Again just use a figure that is consistent with your presentation style.*

At this point the person will do one of three things. They will object. They will say, "How do we proceed?" Or they will think about it and mull it over. For the most part if you have presented in a way that mitigates objections and designed the policy to fit their goals you will move forward and close the sale.

Remember the person sitting across from you is most likely not a policy wonk or insurance expert. Retouch on key concepts, on the benefits, on a client's goals in perspective to your offer, etc.

Closing the Sale.

The simplest way to ask someone for money, is by asking them for money. "How would you like to pay?" Or, "John, the life insurance company made you a great offer, from what we discussed it fits your budget and most important of all it protects your family…. How would you like to pay?" And then shut up and wait for answer.

Again everything up to this point has more or less been placing a lot of responsibility on the prospect to make the correct choice or protecting their family. It builds a tremendous amount of trust. But, it's different from what other price driven sales people tend to do and most people appreciate that. As an expert you guide a prospect through the process not shove a solution down their throats.

Chapter 11: Summation

Learning is a process, experience alone is not a sufficient indicator that wisdom has been created. Thanks for taking the time to read this book. If you enjoyed my book please leave me a review it would greatly help me distribute this knowledge back to the industry that I love so much. There is a tremendous amount of change in our industry, and I hope this gave you something worth reading.

Appendix of Questions

Prospecting Questions
1. What do you do for a living?
2. How long have you been doing that?
3. What do you enjoy about it?
4. What do you do really well? (With your job)
5. How did you get into that (activity/job/company)?

Transitioning Questions
1. Who handles your life insurance?
2. Who do you currently have your life insurance with?

Opening Questions
1. How can we help?
2. Before we get started John, what kind of questions and concerns did you have?
3. How do you feel about spending some time to sit down and make sure your coverage is current?
4. So, besides price, what is important to you?
5. How confident are you that your savings will last all the way through your retirement?

6. When your great grandsons talk about you, what do you think your legacy will be?
7. "What kind of specific questions and concerns do you have?"
8. "John, why are you looking for life insurance?"
9. "Have you purchased life insurance before? What was the experience like?"
10. "How can we help?"
11. "How fast did you want to start protecting your family, today or tomorrow?"
12. "Assuming we could find you the plan that fit your budget, was enough to protect your family and with the right insurance company, would you want the policy to start immediately?"

Needs Analysis Questions
1. How did you arrive at $500,000 of coverage?
2. Have you purchased life insurance before? (To explain process).
3. Since you last purchased your policy 10 years ago, how has your life changed?

4. How often do you want to review your coverage to make sure it's current?
5. I noticed that your policy only covers you for ten years, can I ask why?

Closing Questions
1. How would you like to pay?
2. Would you like to pay with a credit card or bank account?

Other Books

- How to Sell Life Insurance.: Life Insurance Selling Techniques, Tips and Strategies Jan 27, 2018
- How to Sell Indexed Universal Life Insurance: Using a Supplemental Life Insurance Retirement Plan. Feb 19, 2018
- How to Sell Property and Casualty Insurance.: Understanding Insurance Sales, Tips and Techniques. Feb 3, 2018
- How to Sell Indexed Universal Life Insurance. : Using a Supplemental Life Insurance Retirement Plan. Second Edition Dec 8, 2018
- How to Sell Annuities: Annuity Sales Techniques, Tips and Strategies. Mar 12, 2018
- How to Start and Build an Insurance Agency. Edition 2: An Insurance Agency and Brokerage Guidebook. Jul 30, 2018
- How to sell Annuities. Second Edition: Annuity Sales Techniques, Tips and Strategies. Jan 13, 2019
- The Great American Protection Crisis of 2034: Pension Maximization Using an Indexed Universal Life Policy May 31, 2018

- How to Sell Auto and Home Insurance: A guide to Qualifying and Presenting. Mar 25, 2018
- How to Start and Build an Insurance Agency. Edition 2: An Insurance Agency and Brokerage Guidebook. Jul 31, 2018
- "I only smoke when I drink...": Easy ways to have hard conversations as a life agent. Jan 2, 2019
- How to Sell Indexed Universal Life Insurance.: Using a Supplemental Life Insurance Retirement Plan. Second Edition Dec 9, 2018
- How to Sell Umbrella Insurance 2nd Edition: A guide to qualify, present and close. Jan 15, 2019
- How to Sell Umbrella Insurance.: A guide to Qualify, Present and Close. Mar 18, 2018
- How to Market a Modern Insurance Agency.: New School and Old School Marketing Systems. Apr 29, 2018
- How to Sell Auto and Home Insurance. Second Edition: A guide to qualifying, presenting and closing. Jan 26, 2019

- Insurance Agency Economics: An Insurance Agent's guide to Insurance Agency Economics. Feb 4, 2019
- How to Sell Property and Casualty Insurance 2nd Edition: Understanding Insurance Sales, Tips and Techniques. Feb 13, 2019

www.ingramcontent.com/pod-product-compliance
Lightning Source LLC
Chambersburg PA
CBHW030642220526
45463CB00004B/1606